Heaven Beneath

ALSO BY ANNE MARIE MACARI

Ivory Cradle
Gloryland
She Heads Into the Wilderness
Red Deer

Heaven Beneath Poems Anne Marie Macari

A Karen & Michael Braziller Book   PERSEA BOOKS / NEW YORK

Persea Books, Inc.
90 Broad Street
New York, New York 10004

Library of Congress Cataloging-in-Publication Data

Names: Macari, Anne Marie, author.
    Title: Heaven beneath / Anne Marie Macari.
    Description: First. | [New York] : Persea Books, [2020] | Summary: "From Anne Marie Macari, author of Red Deer, comes a staggering collection of loss and love in the age of Anthropocene-heartbreaking poems rooted in the primordial, the elemental, and the communal"—Provided by publisher.
Identifiers: LCCN 2020009283 | ISBN 9780892555123 (paperback)
Subjects: LCGFT: Poetry.
Classification: LCC PS3563.A2335 H43 2020 | DDC 811/.54—dc23
LC record available at https://lccn.loc.gov/2020009283

Book design and composition by Rita Lascaro
Typeset in Helvetica Neue
Manufactured in the United States of America. Printed on acid-free paper.

First Edition

For Noah, Candice, Luke, Melina, Jeremy & Julianne
And For Suzie

CONTENTS

FOUR

Oh Matchless
Earth, We
Underrate the
Chance to
Dwell in Thee

Emily Dickinson

ONE

Atlantic

I remember you at the helm the day you shouted
of spouts in the distance and within minutes

the giant surfaced alongside our boat—

Space animal in a shroud of baleen   In chalky
memory I see its fluid eye

and silent hull, the terrible slant
of its mouth—a creature climbing, finding us

in open ocean, then staying as long as
a creature can

before diving, irretrievable, the boat rocking
on a blank surface   Now I carry

its missing bulk invisible beside me, you

older than I ever imagined, speaking
through water, half-

submerged between the diving and rising, one lid
drooping, and the air

around us glassy and wet

Natural History

Then, placing the Blue Grosbeak alongside
scissors, forceps, cornmeal, and cotton,

he spreads the chest feathers, running
the razor down the bird's breast

to separate skin from muscle, speaking
quietly as he rubs membrane from

the thick pectorals once used for flying—

And if some believe the soul is a bird,
then this is the soul dissected,

caressed inside with cornmeal
to absorb all moisture,

heart and lobed liver preserved for DNA—

He pulls the skin back over the skull
to remove the brain, snipping each eye

from its socket, tongue from
throat, anything that could rot—

I don't turn from the slit bird but lean
close when he points to the red sac

with speck-sized eggs—I strain to see past
his hand, stippled

with blood, the beak open wide

like a chick waiting for its mother,
stuffed with cotton, toes spread,

the bone of each wing tied together
in the cavity that's then sewn up,

beak pinned shut
In this room

of dead birds, the feathers
give off such quiet—

Dark matter—

The heavy door closing, lights
switched off

Boats Can Take You

Now I know that nothing is closed —
boats can take you

through a ravine then out
where oily weeds and plastic bags,

cast-offs   I sit in the sun,
I don't know why this earth,

why my body, why daylight,
why bridge and its shadow over water,

a shore where bird prints
get lost in the slap of river,

they repeat but they're not the same

I know less than when I
was young, when the net, rippled

and wet held me, now
my self, less, my mouth and eyes, less —

This time of year, trees bud out
abundantly brief, pink and white wafers

raining down, they are boats sinking
into earth, dissolving, conducting

the black vein of cosmos, black vein
that repeats but is never

the same   I hear sounds the petals
make in dirt, the dogwood's hard

birthing, watery vortexes, I hear myself
breathing behind a far-off door

I Looked and Lo a Lamb

We walked with the lamb with the cloud
on its back, we walked with trees and birds
Each day I start out I don't know
where I am, stay with me if you can

I looked out ahead, I looked below
I looked and lo a lamb was grazing
and teasing the grass with its mouth—
from where does happiness come?

From the side like a gash? A knife
in my ribs? Or a seed under
my tongue? Is it born? Can it die?
Can I call it home? How

does happiness come?
Each day I start out, I don't know
who I am, when you die I will follow
after you—your smile, inward, silent—

Send Something Back

If his absent memories cry
quietly from some place
we cannot hear, if he seems

to be steering through a new
language, if he doesn't go
into the kitchen carrying

bags of lobsters he will cook
and crack with his strong
hands, and if he has no plans

and doesn't rise early to go out
for pastries or drive his
car and if I bend to him now

as I would my own child
and stroke his hair before I leave   Yes,
for years we did not say *I love you*

and when I started saying it
he'd freeze, almost shake,
trying to reply, to lift

the words out of himself   Now
he pauses—practice has made
him stronger, he carefully removes

three words out of the ocean
of words
me   you   more

Florida

Sharp saw grass for miles, pockets
of willow, and in the shallows

ibis and heron wading gluey
water   Finally I'm really

breathing, first time since the day
you stopped walking, sitting

in your blue robe, cashmere throw
tucked over your legs

our only mantra   *body*   *body*   *body*

someone pricking your finger for blood,
studying your swollen feet,

asking you what year, what month?

Beneath the surface, rot bubbles up
through rain-soaked

muck, all this water on the move

filtered through algae, unending sedge—
Shouldn't I have wondered

soul   when you looked at me confused,

haloed by your milk-hair   I want
to travel with you through

the endangered landscape into

the haunted reeds, alarmed
        flocks against the light—

the wild scattering

I Feel the Need of a Deeper Baptism

to be with nettles and thorns
to be with tree stumps, withered fruit,

to be with the drowning dog
Quiet

        don't call their names

I search for the gash in the wall

March Snow

A piano falling through trees, I want

to hold back the broken notes, muzzle what's coming—
Remember his voice?   Without static?

All the old houses come together,
all their conversations, and me

still listening from another room

TWO

Down in the Lowly Vale

Down in the lowly vale
there are stories of

mind demolition
there are roads that cross

with an X through the woods,
abandoned cars in the woods

Down in the lowly vale there's humming,
buildings sing then fall

(Shadow government in
an undisclosed location)

    Couldn't stop shivering once I started

(a cold place in the lowly vale)   I asked him
is it protection?   or

is it disease?   True, true

so true so true, said the liar

with great ease

Piero della Francesca at The Met

The leopard-spotted hills spring
to life, I enter the scrim—
Like the morning after the hospital

when I passed a man sitting on
the sidewalk, his back against a building,
his eyes and mine joined

and I slipped out of myself
through him, his eyes
a road I passed through to a view

from above where I looked down
at earth, almost laughing
at our games, then dropped

back inside my body—
Like Piero's renunciate, glancing up
from his book at a pilgrim

hovering with a question—
Having died so many times
why do we still want more?

Singed cry of the leopard
calling us back
to the painted world

Who Will Bow and Bend like the Willow

Fold forward, sapling,
press lips to the earth,
let sight open
inside   Fold close

to your chest
oceans and tides, be still
in the foaming mounds
Who would survive

must bow and bend
like the willow in
throes of fright, swabbing
gravel and snapping

its head, afraid
of losing its mind
I come to the tree,
and fall through

the roots, I can't say
where I'll land, I can't say
where my body
will rest, I hope I'm not

losing my mind
Who would survive
must bow and bend
in oncoming throes

of light, whipping air
and dragged in dirt
a tree half out
of its mind

Everglades

*"river with a valley so shallow it is measured
in inches"* says McKibben

and no longer   *Ever*   but shrinking,
this marsh-wealth in a buzz

of conversing, wing flaps and wind, ringed
by housing, drained by canals,

an expanse thick with mangroves, orchids,
birds erupting out of grasses—

*"so flat that a broad sheet of water flows slowly
across it on the way to the sea"*—

algae, floating lilies, water purified
and sent into

the dreamscape—   Heaven's

beneath us, what I look down into,
bubbling mud, permeable skin—

Driving here, miles

across paved-over space

till what's missing gathers—
jaw open in the sun,

wings explaining—

What can't be seen is more
than all of this   Strokes

of green blades   swells of nothing—
we're   *Ever*

latched to each other, burning

You Came to Me

I dreamed you opening my bedroom door
a child again, eight or ten, you looked

like my son, hair dark over your brow
I said, *You can't come in*

Along a gravel path, we walked toward
the water's edge

I pointed across, *You have to go—*
What kind of woman

am I?   Brother, swim
across the blue lake, though I can't

see
           the other side—

Swim, arms hurt pulling the soul,
arms hurt hauling the soul

Train

Take me out of the new century, there's
a train will go there, backwards, passing among

trees that look ready to burst into flame, past
stone walls giving off baked mineral smells—

I wait for the call—guttural bird settling
in the tall California oak—I'm drinking water

in the land of drought, where someone's
digging for elixir to soothe a sun-sick

mind   I want to unhistory myself—

train out of here—as if none of this
ever happened, the thrumming wings

flying backwards, searching for rain

I Never Did Believe

At night, we go to sleep
and die, we fall down
the sliding hole

at night we go
to sleep and die, deep
down the dreaming hole

Come through, fast,
so we can know
one more day

or a spider's thread
might grab us, bind us
in the hiding hole

I never did believe
but I practice
each day—what

is real is also not
when diving in
the sleeping hole

Story with no start,
dream without end,
it calls me through

draws me home,
deep down
the drowning hole

Alligator

Once armored and scaly, now
bloated, with a wry smile,

the dead alligator

is guarded by vultures
who won't be scared off

Chalky ghost, tilted
in a ditch, legs stilled

along its flank as if mid-step
in a procession, ready

to plod onto the highway—

We walk around it to the wooded
path soaked and foggy

from last night's rain, roots
combing out through mud,

wet branches low hanging
and soon I'm paralyzed

in heat and overgrowth, swatting

insect clouds and webs
wanting to turn back through

the wet slab of air, to be released

onto the roadside with its stench
of gator—

Early morning haze rising, blank
tarmac crossing

the river of grass

Yielding and Simple

Don't go down into heaven, don't go down
to heaven's woods, where
deer lead the way into circles

of birch, through circles and shadows, too fast
to follow   Linger where decay
opens to our steps, where we cleanse ourselves

with dead leaves   Could I ever
be yielding and simple?   Yielding
and simple again?   Different than

before? O dear one, don't go down
to heaven while I'm still learning   Spiral
forest, no path through the brush

Heaven's in the voices, quick through
branches, voices yielding,
simple, through circles of birch

I Feel the Need of a Deeper Baptism

Voices in all directions,
V formations overhead—
sand opening below

my feet, sea change
in the tow—I feel the need
of a deeper baptism,

to be in grass with gulls,
to be with the meat
inside the shell, to live

in spiral shells—
I feel the need of the hole
in sand that froths

when water's called back
and under the weed,
silver green, many things

live on that

Narrow Tunnel

Dying bird convulsing
singing a squeezed-

out tune, shuddering
on hot cement

What could I do?

Will it fly a narrow
tunnel, meet

on the other side?
Like the morgue's

back room awaiting
the dead to arrive?

We must be meek, is that
what we're taught?

Or humble? Patient?
Subsumed? Taking leave

with a squeezed-out sound?

No feathers have I
No cure   I tell you

I have no cure, the children
go down with wings

akimbo, pecking
an unseen dome

THREE

Hummingbird Bones

in a small box, in a museum cabinet,
legs fine as white hair, I think

of all the beings pinned to boards, I think

of bird-ghosts swooping around

this basement and bones
chewed clean

by flesh-eating beetles—

The child makes a nest of her palm—
any body can be a nest, any corner, cliff,

any music flying from the radio—

I want to say I'll come back
in a state of torpor, I'll try

to speak but won't be able

to move my mouth to tell you
how perfect the bones and the hand

that holds them, the eye-hole

full of memories of flight,
of ecstasy in flowers'

throats, wings beating
so fast they disappear, its brain

a sapphire tunnel—

There's a room of metal cabinets,
there's a hand holding bones,

all around us a shuddering—

There's a nest for the body,
made of cardboard

and light

Children

Walk the grace-line

    walk barefoot in grass

no one's property this earth

    but flows through the shaft

of your legs and down

    into root into rock

When you wade in water

    when kneel in muddy pools

speak with seeds rocks trees

    to chanters with wings

in your ears

With a New Tongue

In through my ear, in
through my mouth

inside my cavern and cup,
under the fingernail's

tender pink slit, in
the black holes of my eyes—

When I wake, short
is my day, I wake

then fall back asleep
When I wake my dream

goes abroad, I chase
as it floats far off—

With this new tongue
I'm trying to speak, it's heavy

and lolls in my mouth,
I'm working to speak

with my new tongue
of steel, so heavy the sounds

slip out   In through
my mouth, in through

my ear, in through
the space in my hair,

invisible swarms
approaching, mechanical

herds of the air

Down in the Lowly Vale

Who brought us here,
and why did I go along?

I think my eyes are made of paper
and all their images

powder and ash   To survive means
others will not

But the ice?
The blue ice and its calves?

Down in the vale even microbes
going extinct, and no more bats

no wild flights at dusk

In my head a roar
as when I was a child and put

a sea shell to my ear expecting

a message   Droning vale,
roads snaking—

Now we lay us down,
in the valley,

in the lowly vale

Bow Down

to the hospital bed, to the sleeper,
his mouth open wide

Bow to breath uneven,

to the deaf man on the curtain's
other side   Bow

to a fear of tight blankets—
pills, needles, blood,

buzzing ceiling, metallic
glare   Here

in this processing center,
clear fluids in plastic

tubes—

Bow down to limbo's
white light, quiet feet

down the hall
passing through

Hospital

To swim in a pond of milk,
to sink, an old coin,
to drink from a pond
of milk—this is the path

slow strokes in white darkness
not knowing up or down,
wake or sleep—

You in the middle
of the pond, lost
in swells of foam,

not even calling out,
who never
learned to swim

Who Do You Love?

As seed is mixed in soil
As bone is mixed in blood
As an eye is mixed in clouds and sleep,
I am mixed with what I love

I hear a hum, simmering
in my head, spinning
melody, refrain
of soul   Who do you love?

I love the one of root
the same as one of sky
and one is one in skin
and stone, shadow same as sun

I can't see past the window
Something like light, but not—
A wave in glass, a shifting ray,
fragments speaking in glass

I practice, Friend,
to see you whole, with light
inside your limbs, a shade
passes across your eyes

will it leave, or settle in?

Come Life

A grain of sand in my womb
rubbed and grew in me, pearl

of hair and bone, inkling
of spine   Like a swollen moon

I phased, I phased till full,
till a child revealed himself

outside the diamond hold
Come life, closer, through

the orchard zone, from rooms
of otherness   from wider

than wide   Jellied seeds
in corners, odors

of the void, enter when
our backs are turned

nesting in our blood

I Feel the Need of a Deeper Baptism

I want to return to heat, to storm-
scarred trees whitened

by salt and wind, to find again,
perched between palm fronds,

the barred owl, feathers swirled
around its large eyes—

I feel a need, a need,
my mind awkward, unmoored,

my mind without a roof

and green fronds like curtains
across my chest—

Along the seed floor, inside
the humus, carcasses

of small creatures decay, microbes
dine—I want to return

to the vault of wilderness
we stumbled on, how

it blinked back at us

where we stood at the border
of the trees, beneath

the bright, beating sun

The Room

Tonight, snow intermittent, flakes
flat as ash or

anything broken and raining down—volcanic, atomic—

I move through midnight, then 2am, books
stacked, my glass of water—

Behind clouds, a white blur, the ghost ship
half sunk or half risen

riding quiet to the other side

Awake, within my walls, I'm as alone
as I long to be

in the complete, in the nothing

that carries me, drifts me—

Book, drown me
Water, dream me
Table, knock me
Lamp, flame me

I'm yours now, lost
witness, forgotten
blessing

I Couldn't See

Clouds, layered and lit, sailing
above the tops of buildings

the way herds must have passed

across plains, owning the earth
when all wild was wild

and we were herds ourselves—

Last summer, hiking up north,
we broke off twigs with clusters

of blueberries and grazed
as we walked, bringing

branches near our mouths, pulling

fruit off with our teeth
And I felt young again in the old forest,

and felt old having carried
these memories across

the sprawling continent seeking

trees and open water,
finding animals in their rightful

homes   Since the loss,

I'm unwinding the wire
wrapped around my body,

I couldn't see it—

I hurt everywhere, hard
to breathe, to sleep, hard to move

through the saturated air—
Rising, we skirted warm bear scat,

passing trees older
than ourselves, climbing extinction's

ridge to where the view opened
through spruce and hemlock,

the forest shifting, moving
around, beyond us

FOUR

Humpbacks

We're small now, small
as fish in our tiny school, kayaking

toward booming spouts,
flukes and shadow-backs

breaking the glassy sea—

All around we see, hear—whale—and drift
reckless to encounter them rising,

ethereal tons unstitching

the surface—the sea a netherworld

I dream into but can't know, where
a fin rises like a black door

then disappears

I've come here to be lost
in the blue center, rocking

on the brink of wet
darkness, sea

swelling with beings,
two miles out

waves picking up

Where is the Gem?

Who knows red
or cobalt

or the minerals
in my head

emerald stain
of hummingbird

purple tinge
of dread?

Where is the gem
that was promised?

Crystal in silt and clay
or the spark in

the tree as I come close
and it reaches

then bends away
My red tree didn't

ask to bloom, didn't
pray not to shrink

in the cold, the gem
of its veins runs

wild through its tips
ruby through its tips

it touches me
then pulls away

Tidal

Twin Meadows, Alaska

Briny flats and mist—a water-world tilting
empty then full, now empty

again, with its sucking music,

barnacles that hiss along the waterline,
seaweed and milkwort exposed

What a boggy sponge we stand on
when we're not balancing

on the cobbles, when we take to the starry moss
spread across the sea meadow,

aiming for the green tree-line—

Something's urging me down
out of myself, into the dark drink

of peat, brown roots, gray sand, urging me
to crouch in the grasses   like a snail

or cluster of berries

I'm the one who knows how to leave
on my own   Without saying goodbye

I hold the rye-grass in my hand, stroking
its braided head

I want to take my shoes off, I want to make it

to the tree-line, reach
my hand inside

Down to the Deep and Rolling River

I went to wash my soul
I went to rub my face

from the mirror forging
a path through reeds

The meek arise like foam
on the river, they gather

in the stream
The meek rise and float

in the current—the world

is already made
They spread like stars

on the river, in waves
and waves and waves

Down to the deep and rolling river
I went to wash my soul

I went to wipe my face
from the mirror, the world

is already whole

Narrow and Winding

All night searching backwards till
I found her on the ship's log—

Margaret Phair, servant,
from Ireland during the famine

All night DNA boats lighting my bloodstream

      We got up early to drive to Florida prairie
and arrived with sun brimming,

with green swollen spikes

of saltwort around our feet, birds
going silent with

the light, I wanted to draw

that meadow into my blood, to take it back
to Margaret, on the boat, I wanted

to remember what
I couldn't know

      Field of green succulents, you entered me,

your secrets   Tell me
we're not apart from one another, that

the sea-prairie flowers in me

Tell me you know me, that I will return,
recycled—vapor to rain and back,

that I am vapor adrift over

a salt plain, draining into a brown bog,
that my ever-after

is to be broken, dispersed,
swaddled in algae, sucked

into muddy roots, washed
down, drawn up

Narrow and winding path,
devouring insects

herd me through slick air
calling me into the fold

When the Rains Come

I dreamed earth was a pebble inside
a mouth, the stars were teeth
in the maw, I dreamed I walked
in circles, tossed around

Am I worthy?   No,   *Yes,*   No—
a flood of shame soaks me
I go back to the beginning, a pebble
rolling, a mouth in a mouth

in a mouth, back to a beginning
and sucked through the dark,
curled up, a grain in the dark
When the rains come, I'll be

Wash me   Wash me   I'll be
the one ready to shed my skins
When come the rains I'll let go my
feathers   failures—

arms out I'll be   *Wash me—*
a silver note going clear
in rain   *rain*   in the mouth
of the pebble going clear

Thrice Blessed

They slipped a bone
in my head—forgetting
is the greatest good, they slipped

a bone in my head   Blessed,
thrice blessed, or infinitely so

I begin to recall my past

I remember stillness, I remember
milk, I remember someone's voice

There is life concealed

beneath   beneath   snowy bone,
cells that grow
in gratitude before and after

I'm gone   They slipped
a bone in my head

but I surrounded it

with blood, blessed
it thrice   thought on it
and called it my wild love

I Hunger and Thirst

Rivers of souls in
canyons, windows
that cannot see

I came through to
this life and knocked
on doors, who

answered looked
right through me
One day I'll let go

this hunger and thirst
to find you've
been here all

along, I'll step into
the river of souls,
all along, you've been

here, all along—
I ride out the great
hole in my mind,

wondering what true
thirst requires,
when hunger

is real it hollows
your eyes, what is it
I truly require?

I Called to You and You Answered

Grasses as far as I can see
    sloped like a body, long
with a fertile back   Is that

death out there in
    a wheat-colored gown
whose hide was beaten

near enough to paper?
    I called and something just
ran out of my body

out of not just my mouth
    more than my mouth
as if a tongue could stretch

a billowy scarf in wind
    and a voice would follow
rolling out as far as I could see

could hear   I called to you
    and somehow, voiceless
you answered, like the mandibles

deep in grass and the grass
    deep in contemplation
and contemplation something

living   *Remember when we*
    were alive? you asked
in my mind, and you laughed

and I laughed at the same time
　　because what did that mean
when we were *alive*—

you wanted our voices
　　to meet out there　　You said
I'm trying to find out where I am

We Will All Go Home with You

As a child, picking through
blackberry thickets,
through underbrush

and thorns, I thought
we were all together,
but you weren't born

I filled a pail
with fruit, scratched
my arms in that dense

and stopped to place
the black orb
on my tongue   Far into time,

my mouth a place
of sight, and a purple
black unrolling inside —

I heard the door
while trees leaned overhead
We will all

go home with you, through
brambles and weeds
That is what they said

Strangler Fig

A leaf oozes white sap on my hand, wounded,
ripped from its book

Once there was no photosynthesis,
no leaves, no way to store sunlight

before plankton, moss, pollen-packed wind

   Here, a palm tree stood, a fig seed
germinating in its canopy, over years

devouring its host, the fig's bark
wrapping around the palm—

   I rub the tree's skin, I want to hold on,
bathed in dirt and rain, visited

by apparitions of wind, crawled upon, roots
dangling from my arms—

   Without fig wasps, there's no

pollination, no fruit,
without the fig's flowers the wasps

can't reproduce

      Didn't I try to give freely? Didn't I
feed you?

Not knowing what else I could do—

Host, or parasite, sometimes
I'm confused   Tell me, to what

do I give myself now, how best
to be used?

I Feel the Need of a Deeper Baptism

to slip into a slice of ground,

to turn over, my tongue

in dirt, to be in holy ground—

Bring elements—iron, tin—bring

stalks without their braids,

for ruts where fog sinks

and insects lay white eggs,

I want to be   unseen,

to study without light, no speaking

till I've swallowed dirt—

Fall down, by loam baptized

where feet of animals pass—

I'm dreaming now of ditches, pits,

closets, holes, voids

Down in the Rolling Deep

Ten rivers below this one
below its silver skin

swimmers we have
never seen

Ten rivers down
and a channel, and tides

that pull and suck
where salt-streams churn

This is the dream I received
down in the rolling deep

where I walked among
dead ships and bells

This is the dream of water
bursting from a crystal core

slipping weights around
my feet and telling me

to sink some more

NOTES

The titles of some of these poems come from Shaker Spirituals and were inspired by a moving production in NYC by the Wooster Group called *Early Shaker Spirituals*. The titles I've borrowed are: *I Looked and Lo a Lamb, I Feel the Need of a Deeper Baptism, Down in the Lowly Vale, Who Will Bow and Bend like the Willow, I Never Did Believe, Yielding and Simple, With a New Tongue, Bow Down, Come Life, Where is the Gem?, Down to the Deep and Rolling River, I Hunger and Thirst, Thrice Blessed, We Will All Go Home With You, Down in the Rolling Deep.* Not all of these hymn titles were from the Wooster production, but most were. I've borrowed only titles, no lyrics.

Boats Can Take You: The line "they repeat but they're not the same" comes from a description by Agnes Martin of her work.

Everglades: The quote is a short description/definition of the everglades by Bill McKibben, from an extraordinary book *Home Ground: A Guide to the American Landscape.*

Narrow Tunnel: In memory of the many children, all over our country, in schools, on the streets, in parks, and in their own homes, killed by gun violence.

Who Do You Love? is for Jane Mead.

I Feel the Need of a Deeper Baptism: The line "where carcasses of small creatures/ decay" is from the book *Dirt*, p. 14, by William Bryant Logan.

*

My deep gratitude goes to those with whom I've had the great joy and privilege to share my work for some time now, especially Joan

Larkin, Jean Valentine, Jan Heller Levi, Judith Vollmer, and the late Jane Mead—you have given me so much.

Thanks also to Elizabeth Jacobson and Chase Twitchell for their insights and friendship.

In memory of Jane Mead—I think of her and miss her each day—her friendship and work have been a deep source of inspiration.

For the Horsewomen, always.

Thank you to my friend, the incredible artist Martha Posner, for the cover image of her installation, Leda, photo by Larry Fink.

I'm grateful to everyone at Persea Books for believing in this work and for giving my books a home, with special thanks to Gabe for his generous reading and editing of these poems.

For my family, whose love is the center of my life, whose companionship on our journeys has inspired me—Noah Musher, Candice Smith, Jeremy Musher, Julianne Albano, Luke Musher, and Melina Giakoumis. Also, with gratitude and admiration for the two biologists, Luke and Melina, whose wealth of knowledge informs some of these poems. For my parents for unending love and kindness.

And for Suzie Eastman, whose unwavering friendship for many years now, has brought wisdom, joy, and adventure to my life.

ACKNOWLEDGMENTS

American Poetry Review: *Boats Can Take You, I Feel the Need of a Deeper Baptism*

Connotation Press: *Where is the Gem, We Will All Go Home With You, Yielding and Simple*

Field: *Bow Down, Hospital, March Snow*

Five Points: *Atlantic, Florida, Tidal, The Room, I Feel the Need*

Illanot Reivew: *Come Life*

Italian Americana: *Train, Alligator*

The Massachusetts Review: *Down in The Rolling Deep*

On the Seawall: *I Called to You and You Answered, Strangler Fig Tree*

Poem-a-Day: *Everglades*

Slab: *Send Something Back*

SWWIM: *Humpbacks*

I am indebted to The Hermitage Artist Retreat for the time and space to work on this book, without their generosity many of these poems might not have been written.